How to Make a Living Outside the System

A Practical Guide to Starting a Black Market Business

By Tarrin P. Lupo

Porcupine Publications

Porcupine Publications

ISBN 978-1-937311-02-5

Printed with the spirit of

To all the agorists out there, working hard to make ends meet in a culture where true entrepreneurship and ingenuity are crushed.

Table of Contents

Chapter 1:

Agorism and other markets

I am author Tarrin P. Lupo and I want to first state that there are a lot of people out there trying to change this system of government from within. While I admire anyone's efforts to take on that task, it honestly amounts to beating one's head against the wall. The fact is, this system does not wish to change. It is an extremely profitable, and protected business to be a politician nowadays and most of them will neither cut themselves short nor keep laws within the realm of "small government".

History has shown time and time again that all governments fail. Not one government on Earth has ever survived its own self-implosion. There are two major red flags that happen right before a government collapses. The first is the removal of the currency from a commodity backed system, like gold or silver. When a government starts printing money out of thin air, backed by nothing but promises, it has put a giant hole in the levy. The printing of non-commodity backed paper money (a.k.a."fiat" currency), is the ultimate power play for politicians. To print fiat money is literally to create wealth out of nothing. The second red flag is the practice of empire building: when a country overextends itself so much that it collapses under its own massive expenses.

You can see great examples of fiat currency and empire building massively accelerating the fall of governments all throughout history, as far back as Alexander the Great and Genghis Khan. One of the best examples is Rome. The Roman Empire survived for a very long time until they went off the gold standard and invaded the rest of Europe. As soon as they changed to fiat currency and went empire building, they quickly collapsed.

I bring this history lesson up because that is what is occurring today in most of the countries around the globe. The United States is the worst example of this. It has been pushing massive amounts of fiat currency into the economy over the last 40 years, and obscenely so over the last 10. This current government has over 700 military bases in 150 other countries. There is no mathematical way this country can survive if it continues to do these two things. The dollar is going to fall shortly, and the Government with it, despite all the magic tricks the politicians do to keep it limping along.

Although it sounds fearful, it is also a big opportunity for the ones who are smart enough to prepare. When the dollar collapses, huge amounts of people will be thrust into a black market in order to feed their families. If you are smart you will already have a successful business set up and running while everyone else is scrambling. When the U.S.R.R collapsed overnight, the people who already had black market businesses made insane amounts of money.

Since the dollar and government have not collapsed yet, chances are you will still have to deal with intrusive and constricting laws where you live. Liberties are getting eaten away more and more every day. Some people still believe you can save the sinking ship and change the paradigm of thinking. Although I don't believe there is any way to save it, let's explore some of the more popular thoughts on that idea.

You might be asking yourself, "How do I do that?" How do we change a system that will never change on its own? One way is to "starve the beast". If you stop handing all of your hard earned money over, then the house of cards will begin to waver. The excessive over-regulation of what might at one point have been a truly free market keeps us from being able to enjoy what we work so hard for. With income taxes on state and federal levels, property and vehicle taxes, sales taxes – even taxes on death – it becomes really difficult to be able to achieve our goals of having a stable, successful life, since one cannot keep what they earn. To make matters worse, that money is used in wealth redistribution schemes that never work in the long term, to fund wars that you don't want to support, to pay forever pensions on a job title that was not meant to be a lifelong career (politicians), and more. No one is really looking out for you specifically. The politicians see you as tax cattle, what you produce is theirs first and you get to live on the remains. Only you can determine how to best prepare for and provide for your needs and wants. So, how do you make money that you can actually keep and use at your discretion? One good answer is black and grey markets.

There are a lot of other books available covering black market businesses, but their offerings are very different from what this book presents. Other books typically focus on how to stay invisible and under the radar; however, this book, while it will have a little bit of that strategy, will focus on a new and better way to do it.

I like to look to nature first to see how it has already solved a problem I am having. There is a great example of this strategy I would like to share. A new form of activism that is also a way to run a black market business is on the rise and having great success. The new way to do it is to become like a poisonous frog with your endeavors. Everyone has seen pictures of those bright yellow and black or neon green frogs that live in the rainforest. They don't even bother with trying to hide in the backgrounds or with camouflaging themselves. Why aren't these amphibians hunted into extinction? These frogs are poisonous, and they advertise that fact to the world with their bright colors.

This is the strategy I endorse and will explain better later in this book. I will teach you how to advertise yourself as being too "poisonous" for the authorities to mess with. There are non-violent ways to convince the local gang of thugs that your business is not worth the time, money and embarrassment you will cause their department if they choose to mess with your way of making a living.

Now the question is, why start a business in the first place? When you're young, the idea is simple. For example, most kids have at one time created a lemonade stand. As a child you stepped outside the system without having to do much at all. You buy the materials, barrow the card table and equipment from your parents and you're in business. Let us say it costs ten dollars to acquire those materials and start selling cups of lemonade. All you have to do is figure out the math! Hopefully, you will make a twenty dollar profit and come out on top. It's that easy; you set up the stand, and you use your sales skills to try to bring in people to buy your product. That was all there was to running that business.

I wonder what your experience would have been like as a child, if you had set up the lemonade stand and a jealous competitor ratted you out to the officials, or the people in your development got mad because you were violating zoning laws? What if bureaucrats then sent men with guns, who called themselves police, to shut you down[1]? I wonder what kind of taste for owning your own business you would have in your mouth after that experience? This is what happens when you try to run a business in the "legitimate" world. And I hate using that word, "legitimate", but that's kind of what it means,

---

[1] Martin, Nicolas S. Government regulations: Lemonade Day gone wrong (LA: Times, May 1, 2011) http://articles.latimes.com/2011/may/01/opinion/la-oe-martin-regulations-20110501

though: the legal world where people are normally doing business.

You have to look at the fundamental reason why people even participate in this broken system in the first place. The biggest reason why they run businesses in a "legitimate" world is to cap competition. Here is what I've personally observed after living in an area without any zoning for a long time, which later decided the community wanted zoning. The first businesses to grow and prosper are able to do so because they don't have to deal with oppressive regulations and fees. The successful companies take advantage of their leg up, and start influencing local politics by donating to campaigns or running for city councils, mayor or boards. They entrench themselves in local politics to reward their friends and punish their enemies. Then they use the power of politics and the force behind government to lock out their competitors.

The newly elected businessmen put all these regulations in place so that if you want to start the same type of business that they're running, you'll have to pay these licensing fees and inspection fees. You'll also have to beg permission for approval of your sign; you'll have to pay sign fees, advertising fees, B & O Taxes, and all this other stuff that the very first businesses didn't have to pay because they were "grandfathered" in. They didn't have to do all this and usually will throw as many barriers as they can in the way to prevent competition. Local politics is actually just a protection racket to keep new businesses from starting up that don't have much money. The new companies can't afford to compete against established businesses that don't face the same costs and rules.

At first, when people start a business, they just want to have fun or, maybe, they're broke and they have to make some money. If you are like me, you simply can't work for someone else and you have been fired from every job you've ever had. That's the type of person who will usually start his own business. What normally happens is they'll go in with a great idea and then quickly get bogged down with bureaucracy. Just try to open a business in most cities and you, too, will see that you can't just open your doors. You have to do two to three months of begging, paperwork, zoning, waiting for meetings, bribing the right officials, correcting some arbitrary code violations - you can't just open up and have a business flowing.

This makes for a tremendous amount of strain, and only someone with a lot of money and patience can afford to not be producing revenue for that long. You also spend a good bit of money on the fines and extortion fees they call "permits" and "licenses" before you ever earn one dollar. So we have to look at this system for what it really it is: a protection racket. This is really no different from paying protection money to a local crime lord so he won't destroy your business. At least the mob boss has the courtesy to be honest about what he is doing, unlike your local government who operates under the guise that it is extorting you to protect the public. If you understand that, you'll see the reason that a lot of people and communities simply ignore all those rules, take a risk and step outside the system. I will not sugar coat it; there is risk, but you can minimize the risk considerably.

This book, as opposed to other books out there about underground economies, strives to address the issues from a liberty perspective. I don't think that your friends, neighbors, politicians or anyone have any right to tell you how to make a living to feed your family. Nobody does -- PERIOD! If you're not stealing, being violent, or damaging someone's property, then you should be able to contract with whomever you want. Any kind of agreement you two or more adults mutually desire should be permissible, no matter what some community or politician says.

So to you activists and entrepreneurs who take the risks, I have dedicated this book, and it is you whom I want to encourage and embolden to start businesses and enterprises. My goal is to share my experiences so that you can avoid some of the big, expensive mistakes I've made and start your own businesses at a near-immediate profit. I would love to see businesses start up in such a number that the state simply can't control them. My goal before I die is to see such a great number of free businesses that folks won't even know what it is like to beg the government for permission to work. I see the first step as an army of free-flowing, small, and especially mobile businesses that can't be pinned down or tracked by the police. To do this would be to put into practice a better system that would remove the shackles of government and regulations.

It's better for you, as a business person, but it's also better for your customer! You can operate so much more cheaply if you remove the sticky fingers of government middle-men from your business. It's good for both parties, it's good for the economy, and it's good for everyone except the bureaucrats that make a living by interfering with you.

8

Chapter 2:

Methods in Markets

So where do we start? The traditional and old way of doing a black market business was to stay invisible. This is not the approach I really recommend, but I will say a few words about it. First we have to talk about privacy. There are lots of different ways to do this. There's a great book by J. J. Luna called *How to Be Invisible* that will teach you how to "disappear". When I was reading it, I was struck by how many things I was already doing, instinctively, not knowing there was already a guide to living and doing business that way! I used to spend a great deal of time studying on how to become invisible, or "disappear", until I found a better way. These days my goal as a liberty activist is to simply live in the open as a free man.

I don't want to have to live in fear; I also don't want to make myself an easy target so that I can be easily shut down, either. So there's a balancing act. That's something that you're going to have to personally decide. Where are you going to come down on this? How free do you want to live? Will you choose to live as free and open as you can, like I do? I don't care if people know that I am running any kind of business. I'm proud to be an agorist. "Agorist" is a fancy word for a person who believes that you should be able to have a free market without government interference, and is someone who conducts business without the use of force and violence. Will you, like me, be a proud agorist and "wear it on your sleeve", or will you stay in the shadows praying you never get caught? My mission in life right now is to encourage this system to grow, so I'm open about it and want to show others it can be done.

The alternative, representing the other end of the spectrum, would be people who are the complete opposite. They succeed so well in their mission to be invisible; you'd never really know who they are. You could have a friend, family member or neighbor who runs an underground business and you might never have a clue. Many folks like this run a business completely anonymously. One can even run a business overseas anonymously, and if they run their business correctly, nobody will ever know who is making what income, including the state.

I'd like to give you a few tips on anonymity in this book, but in the end, it's not what I'm trying to focus on. It's more practical to focus on how to do this without sneaking around. It's a process and can be inconvenient at times. As the economy gets worse, many people will become interested in escaping the system while they still have a regular job, with paychecks subject to taxes, workers' compensation insurance and the like.

How do you transition? How do you go from a life where you're still really tied into the system, everything documented, to one in which you are completely off the books, outside the system, and you're not asking permission to make contracts with other people?

Initially, you can do some things to make it harder for the system to track you and also make it easier for you to "disappear". One small step is to get a private mail delivery box, such as a UPS box – do not get a government Post Office box. The beauty of private mail delivery boxes is that they have real addresses. This will assist you, at least at a superficial level, in appearing as if your mail deliveries go to a real residential address. Most people on the planet have no idea where I live; they just know my private mail delivery box. This is the way I prefer it, for simple privacy reasons and not just for privacy from the government. There are crazies out there, people who stalk, etc., and you don't want to make it easy for them to harass you.

You can develop this tactic further; you can use another name to further draw the shades against prying eyes. There are a myriad of ways to get around barriers to privacy. You can bribe your way in if you have to. You can also purchase defunct or abandoned companies. There are people who will sell you crashed companies. My favorites are LLCs (or Limited Liability Companies). All you need is the paperwork and you can set something up pretty easily, without your name ever being on it.

Whenever you set up your private delivery address, one of the best ideas is to use the name of this old company or someone else's name. Just pay someone to go and set it up in his or her name, be it is someone you trust or someone that you don't even know. A great way is to use an indigent person who does not even know your name. It could be a quick thirty or forty dollars for someone down on their luck. Give them the money and watch as they set up a box under their name, then they hand the key and the box account information to you. It all depends on your risk tolerance level. There are many different ways of doing it, whether you're using someone else's name, the name of a "ghost" corporation or a corporation you can't be connected to. You can pursue this idea much more deeply to learn how this is done, but at least not using your home address for any reason is the simplest thing you can do. Repeat, DON'T use your home address. For anything, even voting. Make it harder for people to locate you. Make them do a little bit of work to find you and whatever you're doing.

The next thing I want to cover is the use of banks and bank accounts. Sometimes you have to use banks. Let's say you want to run a business through PayPal, Bit Coin (a new unregulated virtual currency) or you want to take checks. There are different levels of privacy. Some people

refuse to interact with banks at all. There are people who
will keep a bank account solely for their agorist business,
in which they keep very little money, maybe as little as
$500.00. Then, if someone steps in, either a government
agent or an identity thief, only a small amount of money is
vulnerable. Most of their money is sitting, hidden,
somewhere at home, in cash or precious metals. They'll
have that small account just to be practical. There are also
ways to connect bank accounts to LLC.s or to whatever
business vehicle you're using. Sometimes you can even
buy out someone's failed business or company and at the
same time acquire their bank account. Be sure you're not
keeping too much cash in it. There's a good chance the
former owner is not going to peek into their old account
and wipe you out, but why tempt them.

Also, an amazing amount of transaction power can
occur on those anonymous prepaid Visa gift cards. Mind
you, there are fees and possible inconveniences but you
can run an entire business through it if you learn how.
There are different ways to handle it. This tactic might
not be for everyone. Again, you'll have to take your own
personal risk tolerance into account.

There are even ways to start a corporation without
any names involved at all. However, I'm not going to go
in-depth about it here because I want to emphasize that
you should go completely outside the system, and creating
a legally licensed corporation is just reinforcing and
working inside the government system.

I am going to take you through practical steps to get
to where you need to be. As I discussed earlier, the first
small step is to protect your identity. Next, as far as banks
go, if you really want to step outside the system, you
should reduce or eliminate your use of banks as much as
you can. The more of a paper trail you leave, the more of a
target you are. The solution is to live and work in a cash-
only lifestyle. This will be a lot more inconvenient than
you are used to. You'll have to deal with establishments

like check cashing services. You'll also automatically lose some business because some customers won't deal with you if you don't accept credit card payments. The flip side is that you'll have complete privacy and anonymity. Cash is still king.

Let me now point you to businesses that are cash-run and cash-oriented. Hopefully this will give you the impetus to start a cash-run business or you'll use these ideas to convert a business of your own to a cash-only business. I also wrote another book that relates to this, called Stash Your Swag, which teaches you how to properly hide stuff, including cash, that is normally a security risk to keep at home. The book teaches you a variety of free ways to creatively stash whatever you'd like to hide by finding lots of little places to conceal your cash or valuables. This allows one to spread the risk for theft and detection around. There are over a hundred ideas in that book, including ways to hide even bigger sums of cash from bad guys. You can find it at www.Lupolit.com or www.Smashwords.com.

I want to talk to you about why you can't use banks, financial accounts and other institutions and figures inside the system. You'll find it's completely the opposite of running a business in a way that you're used to or have experience running. The fewer books and records you keep the better. You want to make your company run off "disorganized chaos". You should use a system in which your entire books are as complex as an envelope of cash! When you're out of cash in such a system, you're broke. You need to go old school and operate your business more conservatively. You're not going to be able to "play it big" and borrow money like a big business operating inside the system would. I remember a time when banks would give a $50,000 line of credit to anyone who could breathe, but for anyone outside the system those days are over. You're going to have to start slowly. The cool thing about this old school system is that it eliminates debt, reverting to a system of doing business that pre-dates credit. You're

going to use cash for everything. It's a great common
sense approach to keep you out of trouble, and it's also
more realistic. It's just a little slower. You trade speed
and credit for safety, privacy and freedom.

Why, you may now be asking, can't you trust
banks? Banks and accountants will sell you out, that's
why. Banks will allow government officials instant access
to any account you have, for any reason they desire. The
bank officials are instructed by the government agents to
not even tell you that your information has been accessed,
and to openly deny and lie about it!

In my experience, even if you're not "guilty" of
anything, I've repeatedly seen government agents lock
down all accounts of a business or individual. The agents
seize your assets, and you end up going through years of
legal battles to get back that which was yours, at your
expense! You must then protect yourself against these
kinds of consequences. The best way to do that is to not
get involved with banks in the first place.

When you run an underground business, you very
rarely get in trouble with bureaucrats. Fortunately for
you, bureaucrats are lazy! They prefer not to have to
chase anyone down and do the hard work involved for
just a "little fish". They'd much rather have competitors
or neighbors snitch you out and do the detective work for
them. That's what they're counting on. They want the
case to be brought to them on a silver platter; only then
might they dig their teeth in and go after you. Again, the
degree to which you employ these approaches will vary
with your tolerance for risk.

To re-cap, the old school way is to be completely
invisible, where barely anyone knows you're running a
business, which is a low risk way. Putting as many layers
between your actual identity and the identity of your
business as possible is very safe, but complicated. But I
try to encourage people to be open about running a
business while at the same time making it hard for the

state or financial institutions to deal with you at all. Make it so if a bureaucrat does come after you, they're not going to easily find anything and you're not going to cooperate with them at all. Bring such a negative, publicity and/or media storm down upon them and whatever agency rock they climbed out from under, that they just back off and leave you alone.

An example of this would be what happened in Savannah not too long ago. There was a restaurant business that proudly ran without any licensing or zoning. They cooked in their family kitchen, and then delivered the food. They were openly running their business "illegally". One of their customers who worked for a competitor got mad about an order and decided to snitch them out. The detectives set up a sting, wasting their time and taxpayers' money. The Garden City Police Department used five cops in this sting to catch this one business selling their illegal biscuits and gravy. I've got a whole report online at youtube.com/LCLReport, if you'd like to watch the video. Just search "Biscuitgate".

Because there's an existing network of independent media, the story got massive press. The police department was so embarrassed about it (since other agorist businesses and liberty activists made such a stink about it) that the police then made a statement that, even though the Last Biscuit was operated illegally, they were not going to press charges and would let the matter drop. For a while, Savannah's Last Biscuit worked in Savannah without any fear of licensing fees, or any fear of bureaucrats harassing them, because the bureaucrats are scared of the media!

The police department had given the Last Biscuit a free pass to operate unmolested. Their competitors were now pissed off, since they continued having to pay all the extortion fees and all the so-called "business licensing" fees. However, if the competitors could just adjust their perspective it would be to their benefit. "If this lady did it, then our business could do it too!" Sadly most of the businesses were too scared to ever stand up and copy the same tactic.

There is a cautionary tale with Savannah's Last Biscuit, though. Although the Biscuit was now free to practice their business without getting arrested for it, the police were still embarrassed and wanted to find a way to arrest the owners. The owners were wanted for some other old crimes in their personal lives that had nothing to do with their business. The police used those old, personal crimes to arrest and jail the owners. The local government shut the business down by proxy through the arrests. I hope we learn from their mistakes. If you want to publicly challenge the cops in your area, keep your nose clean. Don't give them a backdoor through which to take you down. You have a much better chance that the police will leave you alone if the only thing they can arrest you for is your agorist business.

This story could, and should, stand as an example and inspiration to people that they too can break out of the system and be free. Instead they're going to whine and cry that they're victims of the system. And yet they don't have enough courage to stand up and break out themselves!

This shows you how and why there are two ways to do it. Make yourself invisible if you don't have all your ducks in a row and you've got too much to lose. Or, you can be open about it, defiant, and you will rally other liberty activists around you who will point a huge spotlight on the corrupt system. Many times the bureaucrats will just go scurrying away from the cameras as fast as possible, like they did in Savannah when they first targeted Savannah's Last Biscuit.

The next thing I want to talk to you about is how to choose what business to be in and how to get into it. Then we're going to talk about different methods and media that you can use to promote your business.

Chapter 3:

What to Do

Your first consideration is this: what kind of business do you want to run?

One of the many ideas I will present to you will resonate with you or be a launch pad for your own creative idea. It's important to know that if you're a liberty activist, it's actually safer to do things in the open – once you have some back-up. When possible, ground your business in the existing liberty community and organizations. If you don't already have activist friends, get involved with social media! Sites like Facebook, MySpace, Meet Up and other boards provide a virtual community bringing together geographically far-flung people of like mind. One great site, http://agorism.info is a great primer in free-market-anarchy, promoting the freedom of the Agora (originally a Greek word meaning "market-place"). The site provides multiple examples of using what amount to black market techniques in direct action to change – hence the motto, "Anarchy! Agora! Action!" or "A3". Even Craigslist is prime internet territory for the independent contractor to connect with people willing to do business apart from the meddling of the state. Surrounding yourself with even a virtual community of like-minded individuals allows you to have both a market-place and a consumer base. They will support you if you will support them.

I always go to my list of black-market entrepreneurs first, and give them first crack at any business I want to do, even if it costs me more money. It is an investment in a community that in turn supports me.

If I ever get in trouble, I know they have my back. Additionally, you get the satisfaction of supporting independent family businesses. I want to see them do well and escape the rat race too. For me, it's not just about making a buck outside the system; it's also about encouraging others to break out of the system, too.

So, are you going to employ a skill-set you already have in this new business, or will you acquire new skills to better your chances? Just using the skills you already have is sometimes enough to launch a small side business and begin your black-market entrepreneurism.

For example, if you do computer repair for a private company or the government, put an ad on Craigslist advertising the same or similar services and you can very easily get your feet wet, little by little, without having to abandon the safety net of full-time employment all at once.

We've already seen how you can start a delivery restaurant and generate a lot of instant cash. You can also start a business selling herbal teas with a small herb garden right in your own yard. Expand your knowledge base a bit and you can add natural remedies, seed banks and exchanges. You can also sell plant cuttings at the flea market or even become a small nursery. It is very satisfying to work right out of your yard in what used to be a tiny herb garden but has grown to something amazing! There really is no limit to ways you can make a living as long as you can think of something new to do.

Other examples:

Dog Grooming

Tree Removal (and landscaping/lawn care)

Seed Banks/Plant sales/Plant nursery

Web and graphic designs

Information Technology (sales, repair, consulting, programming)

Pet Care/Pet Sitting

Photography

Carpentry/Construction/Painting

Chimney Sweeping and Repair

Masonry

Gun Smithing

Roofing

House Cleaning

Artisan craftwork (jewelry design, watch-smiths, other trades)

Artists

Tattooing

Food products, brewing, smoke products

Clothing design and production

Although these occupations are service-oriented, almost anything can be turned into a black- market business with some small adjustments.

If your occupation is more highly regulated, your risk of detection and harassment is higher. In dealing with things like alcohol, tobacco (and of course, firearms), government regulation and interference has made both the risk of harassment by goons greater, and the price of the regulated product higher! Prohibition has never worked and people will always find a way around it for a profit. Government interference and taxation of regulated and prohibited products has contributed to massive problems and astronomically inflated cost for people doing business in these industries.

Government interference seeks to countermand the sovereignty each individual has over his or her own body; liberty says you own your life and your body. You should be able to do whatever you want to your body, eat or ingest anything you so desire as long as it doesn't endanger others. The Government says, "I'm going to get in your way and make money (diverting your revenue) while I'm doing it."

As long as any participating human beings are in a mutually consensual contract or agreement, they should be free to engage in any activity that they desire, whether for fun or profit. Stripping, prostitution in all its forms, the purchasing, selling and using of drugs – all these activities which the state calls criminal, a person should be able to engage in without fear of being locked up in a cage. Mutual consent should be the guiding principle between sovereign adult individuals. I don't really care what other people are doing, and I don't want others to care what I'm doing, either. It comes down to one very basic question, do you own your body or does the government? If you own it, you should be able to put anything you want in it.

The higher risk and the socially frowned upon professions will want to use a combination of the privacy techniques and the open activism style. Keep your business invisible but support the activist community. If you support them, they will support you, even if it is socially unpopular.

Of special note here is that if you're going to engage in occupations like prostitution, you have to take special precautions to shield your identity and your location for safety from overzealous clients too. Did you know cops can "legally" do anything they want to a prostitute like even having sex with them first? Yes, sex workers are treated like second-class humans and authorities abuse their civil liberties with frightening frequency. Using pre-paid or disposable cell phones or free Voice Over Internet

Protocol ("VOIP") phone communication software like Skype can help you avoid detection and keep you free from harassment from uniformed thugs ("law enforcement", the Vice Squad, etc.).

I have a friend who has a black market cigarette manufacturing business. He buys the tobacco cheap, rolls the cigarettes mechanically, and sells the cigarettes. Without all the taxes and regulatory costs, they can market and distribute the cigarettes for less than half the price of "regular" tobacco products. They maintain very high quality ingredient and manufacturing standards to assure that their product tastes just as good and is as satisfying a smoking experience as a name-brand smoke. That's pretty bold, not just because of risk of harassment from the Bureau of Alcohol, Tobacco and Firearms, but from a moral standpoint. Why not buy cigarettes from people you trust? As long as they are not saying that they are licensed by the state, or have passed government inspections. You have to be honest about your business. The only people who will rat you out are competitors and busy-bodies. That's why you try to keep yourself anonymous to an extent. Or, as some well-supported activists do, go ahead and make it public and do it in the open. If you are sick of hiding, go ahead and let them find out about you, then just make such a public stink about law enforcement or government goons that they'll leave you alone.

These occupations are classic black-market businesses, and much can be learned and applied by studying how they operate. There's obviously much higher risk associated with these occupations and businesses, but they have a correspondingly higher rate of return as well. In discussing this very phenomenon with another activist named Libertarian Lady, I discovered that exotic dancers can make incredible incomes. Almost all dancers decide not to declare to the I.R.S. So, if you're not hung up on the body and sexual issues that go with the adult entertainment industry (and can handle the psychological and emotional trials that often go with being a stripper), you can make a very robust, cash-only income this way.

Bartending and restaurant service jobs (waiting, serving, busing tables) are also great ways to make and then hide income. I even had an independent bartending business for a while! We'd put ads up on Craigslist and sure enough, once or twice a week, we'd have gigs! I'd charge $25.00 an hour (with a four-hour minimum) to bartend a party, and easily undercut the competition by operating outside of the system – which is always much cheaper. It's riskier, since operating this way does expose you to possible fines and regulations, but it was worth it to me. It's almost always better, if you're willing to assume the risk, to work outside the system and simply pay the fines if you get caught. Or, if you're an activist, resist! Take it to trial and cost the state as much money as possible. Many times they will not go all the way to trial and dismiss your case because it is too expensive to prosecute. The state usually does not want to spend $5000 to collect a $500 fine. Even if they find you guilty, don't pay the fines at all and use it as a form of civil disobedience. Either way, it's cheaper to pay the fines than it is to go through all the coerced licensing. Some people will refuse to pay the fines, do the jail time, come right out and start again! It all depends on who you are.

Chapter 4:

Locations

I'm a fan of the black markets that are already in existence. Look at the immigrant community for inspiration. Immigrants employ their own micro-societies which contain free markets. Go to any ethnic enclave and observe. They speak their native language (a great tactic for keeping communication more private!), they are in a concentrated geographic locale such as a neighborhood, or networks of neighborhoods, and they do business with each other. They patronize one another's health practitioners and they buy their food at one another's stores. In almost every case, certainly in the case of every immigrant I've personally known, all their dealings (or as many as are deemed safe) are off the books. Most don't even take credit cards or checks. It's all cash.

As such, these communities have created underground economies which are already strong. If you take the effort to learn another language, like Spanish, it can allow you to plug into these micro-societies. Get a little acquainted with their culture and you will see these are often some of the finest human beings you'll ever meet and they would be happy to do business with you. Those doing business outside of the system are often high integrity business people; the more established they are, the more they depend upon evading detection by operating fairly and in a way that benefits their community. The market quickly figures out a way to regulate itself.

One of the easiest ways to find an underground economy is to go to flea markets. Flea markets, the business owners, and customers that patronize them, represent one of the last bastions of the true free-market economy in the U.S. What I mean by this is that unlike brick-and-mortar businesses, you don't need a business license or a tax I.D. You just pay rent on a table and can sell damned-near anything you want, and the free market determines your success! If you're trying to sell something no one wants, you won't make any sales. If you sell something people want, you're going to do really well.

If you're highly educated, you might feel as if working in a flea market is "beneath you", but remember, this is about freedom. If you don't mind the sacrifice of working two days a week, on the weekend, to escape the rat race, you can earn an income that can set you free. Sometimes you need very little, even zero cash to start up. Have a garage sale and use that $25.00 or so to buy rent on a table at your local flea market. Look around your house.

How attached are you to all that clutter? Ask yourself: are you more attached to it than you are in love with the idea of independence? Sell it! People will buy anything if you price it right. Leverage your junk! Put it on Craigslist or any of the other free classified sites on the Internet. Put a notice up on your grocery store bulletin board. Then use that money to launch your flea market business.

Once you're at the flea market, look around. Not only are there people selling things at the flea market, there are people offering services like haircuts, nail salons, people giving massages and more. Just know that you have to adjust your pricing when you offer services at a flea market; no one is interested in spending a lot of money. They're motivated by the low prices to attend! Then again, you're spending next to nothing by offering goods and services at a flea market and have nearly eliminated all of your traditional over-head costs. It evens out, even yields a net gain. You could go out and rent a spot at some mall, make a ton of money and then see it all go right back out again as you have to cover your costs.

When you do become an independent businessperson at a flea market (or if you decide to operate inside any other counter-economy), don't forget to patronize the other vendors and services! Don't go to Wal-Mart and buy your groceries, but instead hit that little bodega for your apples! Buy your lettuce from the farm stand at the flea market. Instead of using valuable capital to market to people solely outside of the flea market, put your money and time into that world. Plug in. Plug into the mutual benefit of doing business with one another as well as their vast knowledge base. You will find their collective business acumen of others doing business outside of the state-sanctioned economy impressive. They already know it all! For example: How to stay on the down-low, how to avoid restrictive and expensive laws and regulations and bureaucrats – they've already got it figured out. No need to reinvent the wheel, because this isn't anything new to these micro- societies with flourishing counter-economies.

You can make a very good living while you're getting your feet wet. Then when the economy picks up, you'll be a veteran participant. Before the economy crashed, some vendors at my flea market were making $2,000 a weekend, that's $1,000 per day, just buying and selling stuff at the flea market. Now, you can buy and sell with junk dealers, but I wouldn't buy anything expensive looking for a high return. Don't buy anything that retails for more than $30 or $40. The first thing you're going to do is just clean out and sell your clutter. You've already got two or three months' worth of inventory in your house! Go sell that junk; it's all profit. Don't sell anything you really care about or that you bought at a really high price point. Something you paid $100 for, someone will want to pay $15 for. But if you don't use it anymore, who cares! Sell it.

Another great source of inventory is cheap wholesalers. Buy it for cheap and then turn it around for a profit at the flea market. Businesses that are going under often have inventory that they wish to unload for cheap. They even have wholesale districts loaded with stores in major cities. You can make a hell of a deal on their inventory they want to let go. I got crazy prices by talking to the manger of one of these stores.

Again, all this is cash. Consider your customer when you're selling at a flea market, and price accordingly. People don't want to spend a lot of money at a flea market; that's why they're there! If you're interested in making more money, you can, but there's more of a paper trail. If you want to make more money and take a little more risk then use your smart phone as a credit card machine. I love a device called the square that plugs into your smart phone and acts as a super tiny credit card terminal. It is all fee based and if you link it to a prepaid phone and a ghost account so you can take cards anonymously.

Places like antique malls or consignment stores where you can rent space for cheap, say $100 a month, can make you more money, but to operate under cover, you'll have to rely on those methods of identity shading mentioned earlier. Some of these places keep records of everything you do, and some don't.

Some of them will just hand you cash, and they don't want to know who you are, or what you do, and that's it. Those are the ones you want to find. The more privacy there is, the better it will be. The benefit of using a platform like an antique mall is that the customers are far more willing to dish out cash. The mark-up is totally different, much higher, reflecting the expectation of the customers that they are more likely to find a "treasure". The store will sell your inventory for you; you don't even have to be there. The benefit for them is a steady stream of a variety of different inventories, which is attractive to their customers. If you set yourself up in ten or twelve of these places, you can practically operate invisibly. You just show up, replenish your inventory in your display and collect your money once a month.

Chapter 5:

Using the Internet

You can also make a living buying and selling on eBay. This was really big in the early 2000s. People were just staying at home and making money hand over fist. It's become a lot harder recently as eBay is now referred to by many as "feeBay". eBay and PayPal have increased their merchant fees so much that now you need to mark things up about 15% to cover all the listing fees. If I buy something at $50 and want to double my money, now I have to sell it for $115 instead of $100. To give yourself a little eBay pricing tutorial, go to eBay and look at the "sort" features on the left. Look for the sort category box of "Completed Listings". This will show what people have purchased and at what price.

Let's say I'm selling shoes, and I'm going to buy these shoes from another seller and you've already taken these costs into account. So I'm buying my shoes for $10 and I'm selling them on eBay for $30. I have to also now take into account that 15% of that is going to go right up in smoke, and that if I mark up my product in an attempt to recoup the 15% fee, is anyone going to buy it at the marked up price? So, in order to determine if this is a viable transaction for me to engage in, I'm going to go to the "Completed Listings" section, and I'm going to research and see if people are actually buying a comparable item at that price point. This is an excellent tool. Before you sink a penny into anything, you get to see if it's worth your time.

I made a living off eBay for a year, just turning stuff over from Craigslist to eBay. Plenty of sellers on Craigslist refuse to pay the listing fees on eBay or are intimidated by setting up a seller's account on eBay. Craigslist is wonderful for acquiring inventory to sell on eBay because you can haggle and barter prices down before you buy. You can take anything off Craigslist, say a Star Wars DVD collection, go over to eBay and research the completed listings and see if you can make a profit.

This works really well in a big city, where you can physically go and trade the cash the same day, and there's a big pool of sellers on Craigslist. It's leg-work to go get the stuff, but it's cash. You can turn around and list things right away on eBay that you've just purchased that day! I was making a couple of hundred dollars a day on eBay. It's gotten harder, but if you're willing to do the work and hustle a little bit, it's a really viable way of making a cash living.

Alternatively, you can just make a living on Craigslist, by watching the For Free listings. There are junk dealers who watch Craigslist like a hawk, and when they see stuff coming up for free, they'll drop everything, run on over to get the free item, bring it home and turn around and list it on Craigslist for $30 or $40 and just sit on it. Eventually, they'll sell those items or save them all up and have a garage sale, flea market table or send them to an auction house. I'm sure you've seen people do this with yard sales, too. Yard sales are wholesale paradise, and a great place to buy stuff that you can turn around and re-sell.

You have to be careful, though, if you're buying stuff that you just think will re-sell. My advice is to bring a smart phone or a laptop with Wi-Fi and actually look up that item on eBay (again, in the Completed Listings section) and see what people are willing to pay for it. Let's say you come across what looks like a classic Hot Wheels car. Hold onto it while you look up the price on eBay and see if it's worth it! People get into trouble when they buy things that they like, thinking, "Well, I would pay $20 for this, so will someone else." That's ok if you are your only customer! Otherwise, it's all about what other people (the free market) will pay for that item. So be a good primate, and use your tools! Find out what others will pay before you go acquiring inventory you can't re-sell.

So in near total anonymity, you can set up your eBay account and PayPal account (linked to your ghost LLC or mystery bank account), sit at home, use your private mail delivery box for delivery and shipping, and live completely under the radar this way. As a further benefit, you seldom might have to deal face-to-face with people if others are shipping your inventory to you! If doing customer service makes you feel uncomfortable, this is the life-style for you! If you can't stand people whining and complaining, bitching at you over the phone, buying and selling on eBay might be the way to escape that kind of misery. It's also a great way to start with no money.

Something else at which I've been successful in the past is the creation and marketing of eBooks. You're listening to or reading one of my eBooks right now! I love eBooks, though I'm admittedly not a big reader. I don't buy a lot of hard-cover books, but I do buy eBooks. People over 40 probably haven't purchased a lot of eBooks, but people under 40 feel quite comfortable doing so and buy them in good numbers. The arrival and adoption of eReader technologies like the Kindle, Nook or iPad allow readers to download and read electronic copies of books on these book-sized electronic readers. Over the last three years they have revolutionized publishing.

While downloading an eBook doesn't provide the same tactile experience, the price point of an eBook is so much less than a physical book that consumers are ordering eBooks like hotcakes! And like a physical book, the Kindle reader is portable. But unlike physical book collections that take up a lot of space, the Kindle can be any book you want.

Finally, the aspect that seems to appeal to so many readers is that the book becomes available instantaneously, no waiting. No driving to the book store, no ordering and then waiting. It's instant gratification.

One of the things I really love about eBooks like the one you're reading is that you can follow the links in the eBook right away. And, unlike a real book, authors can edit eBooks on the fly and update them. You can't do that with a "real" book without great additional expense. As an eBook writer you don't have to deal with a publisher if you don't want to! You don't have someone censoring your work, you don't have to deal with running out of copies, and you don't have to risk losing your shirt on books that people may or may not purchase. If you write an eBook that flops, all you've really wasted is your time. You really haven't spent that much to produce the book.

Most people who purchase eBooks realize that they are buying something ten to thirty pages long – they're short – the price point on them is cheap, usually $10.00 or less. The only thing challenging about producing them is the marketing. How do you get people to actually buy these books? There are a variety of ways. You can actually get an online eBook publisher who will take your book and market it for you, and give you a cut of the sale. SmashWords and CreateSpace are examples of this. Let's say you sell the book for seven or eight dollars, they might take two or three bucks out.

There's also a world of online affiliates available, which I will explain. When you go to a website like http://www.clickbank.com you will see that it is a group of private individuals that will agree to affiliate with you, or sell your book on their website for a large cut. This is nothing but found money! In other words, you would have never sold your book, had it not been for their website. You're not doing any of the work to sell the book. Unfortunately, in order for your book to also be profitable to the affiliate, it's going to have to cost (and be worth)

$50 or $60. If you're an expert in your field, this works like a charm! You have to be able to write for a niche that is willing to pay for your knowledge, almost like a consultant, but in book form. Then the affiliate may take as much as a 50% cut – sometimes as much 75%.

Let's do the math again, to give you an example. Let's say I'm using the affiliate to sell my book at a $40 price point. If I offer the affiliate 75% to sell the book, I only get $10, but I'm getting $10 for something for which I didn't have to do any additional work. At this point, the affiliate is doing the hard work! A go-between company, like ClickBank, takes care of all the transactions, all the money, protects both buyer and seller, and acts almost like a broker, to make sure everything is kept honest.

Or, you can copy my model. What I did is create a website with a lot of free information, hundreds of pages of it, but every page ties back into the fee-based product, the eBook I'm trying to sell. This model essentially says, here's a ton of really good information for free, but to get my best stuff, you're going to have to pay a premium. It's a small premium, but a premium nonetheless, and that's your profit. In this model I give a lot of good quality information away for "free" so that I can establish that I'm an expert on a subject. The potential buyer will now trust me enough to buy the very best material.

And I market all this myself. I make a website that gets so many hits it's unbelievable! I should explain about the return on investment in the making of a website here, so that you don't go spinning your wheels making a really pretty website that gets zero hits. I made a website that looks like it was made in 1990 and was designed by a kindergartener, and it gets at least 100,000 hits a month! People would die to get this kind of traffic. The secret is unbelievable: the simpler, the better. The site with the most hits in the world is Google. If you look at Google, it's an empty white screen with a search bar and a couple of buttons. Granted, we're also talking about the utility of a site like Google, which is massive, but your site can be incredibly useful and simple too, and attract huge amounts of traffic as well. Many users still have slow computers and internet connections, and they don't have the time to try and download those pages with fancy flash graphics and audio! Many users bail on pages like that before they've even read a word.

Of course there is more to it than just that. Maximizing a web page for search engines so that they can be easily found is an art called Search Engine Optimization. But I use a little bit of a cheat. There's a website called http://sitebuildit.com that will hold your hand and walk you through developing a website that actually gets traffic. Appropriately, it's more expensive than simply going to http://godaddy.com and making a website yourself from scratch. Any "Joe" can spend $10 and get a domain name, host and a website. Site Build It costs about a dollar a day. With Site Build It, keep your eyes peeled for specials that allow you to set it up for about $100 a year; however, normally the fee is about $300. The tutorial is comprehensive. You make the website a block at a time, without having to know anything about how to do this. The reason I like it is that it really is like a website in a box - it's a turn-key process. They do all the behind-the-scenes busy-work that you'd have to pay a webmaster a half-hour a day to do. For example, when you update your site, it updates your RSS feeds, calls the Google web-crawlers, and all this other stuff that I neither comprehend nor want to spend my time doing. All I have to do is crank content out. It does all the nuts and bolts stuff for me. So for me, a dollar a day is worth it to market my book!

For some reason, the liberty community has a ton of tech-heads in it, who probably will want to build their own stuff. They will probably ignore my advice but honestly, my site will probably get way more traffic than theirs! Their technical expertise exceeds mine, but I know what I'm talking about in terms of marketing and driving traffic.

Or, if you want to make your life incredibly simple, just go to a publisher, give them your book, let them do all the marketing for you and keep cranking out books.

If you're marketing your own books, more than likely, you're not going to make a lot of money at first. You could, but your average book might make you about $20 a day. But over time, this really adds up! Again, you only have to write the book once, and it can go on selling for years and years. Hopefully, you will have many books out there at the same time. If you're going to use affiliate marketing and you're capable of writing something truly unusual, you might make hundreds of dollars a day, and then your book might be phased out. Some writers of books that use affiliate marketing make a ton of money in the beginning, and then after that, purchases of their book drop off. It greatly depends on what your book is about. It's far better to keep it realistic, and know that most people don't write for this affiliate market. Small, non-fiction, helpful books are the easiest to start with. You can make a ton if you have a bestselling novel, but it is extremely hard to get noticed.

The secret is to keep cranking out books! Twenty different books at $20 a day is a real living - real income, residual income. Residual income is very different from a 9 – 5 grind where I work for two months, get my paychecks and have to keep working to get more paychecks. With a book, you work really hard for a short time. You don't make much, but once it's up and running, it continues to make money for you and you never have to do a damn thing to it, if you don't want! It just sits there, and sells, and sells, and sells, and the money slowly trickles in, and it starts to really add up. Could you use an extra $20 a day?! I could! Imagine if you had an extra $400 a day from a bunch of different books!

So eBooks are a really great solution to creating income and freedom. And if you set it up correctly, within a couple of years you could have a lifestyle where you can really be free. You could live anywhere you want in the world, and your account is just filling with money, day by day. It's almost like a retirement plan. It can work out far better monetarily for you, the author, than traditional publishing.

Just to give you a little anecdote, I have a friend who published a book of poetry. It was all over Barnes & Noble for awhile, but she only made about a dollar a book! With my eBook, if I sell it for $6.95, I make about $6.50 after PayPal fees. To make a comparable profit, my friend needs to sell six books to my one! So even though she probably outsells me, conversely, I probably make more money than she does.   Especially because, in the long run, my book will still be actively selling after this print run is over for her. She has to pay for a whole new printing, additional marketing, etc. I don't have to do that. If my book doesn't sell, no big deal, it doesn't cost me a thing. I just have to write a new book!

There are so many benefits to eBook publishing. The two primary benefits are that you can be traveling all around the world, and not be tied down to one geographic location to create income, and that that income is residual.

The last great thing about an eBook is it allows you to experiment. Say you don't want to deal with selling an eBook, well give it away for free and sell advertising sponsorships. Newspapers and magazines have done this for years, but you rarely see it in books these days. I am leveraging the power of FREE! Free is extremely powerful and I expect over the next few years it will be read thousands upon thousands of times. For just, say $25 your potential customer's ad could be seen thousands and thousands of times over the years.

A quick side note, you can make a heck of a lot of money without selling anything at all. I have friends who get tons of hits with their Site Build It websites who don't sell anything. They just use Google Adwords and get paid each time folks click the little blue Google ads embedded in their site. I actually make an additional $200-$300 a month on these little ads and I do absolutely no maintenance on them. If you so desired you could have nothing but large sites with free information and get paid off Adsense and other ad companies like Project Wonderful and Yahoo. If you maintain your ads and watch the trends you can make a ton of money building these kinds of sites.

Over the last year something really huge has developed on the Internet for the black market. These two useful tools will completely change how business is done over the Internet and create a true free market the government cannot do anything to stop.

The first is Bit Coin. Bit coin is an inflation proof currency. Although it is very different from anything else out there, the main things you need to know about it, is it can be used completely anonymously and can't be shut down. Unlike Paypal, Bit Coin is not a centralized company. It is a free, decentralized service that is watchdogged by thousands of its own members. This open source format keeps everything honest and visible at all times. You can find out all the nuts and bolts of how it works by "Googling" Bit Coin.

The second are Tor sites like Silk Road. Silk Road is incredible and will take the black market to the next level. I am not an Internet expert so I am going to explain this very basically. Silk Road is really not a website; it is a hidden service; it's kind of like a black market eBay. You can find everything from black market cigarettes to drugs and guns. You have to use a program called Tor, which allows you to see hidden and secret websites. It is ironic that the CIA created Tor to do nefarious things around the world, but now it is being used as a huge tool for freedom.

So with the combination of anonymous decentralized currency and an anonymous decentralized market place, the world is about to be shaken. The government is freaking out because since there is no website to shut down or no business to go after they can't stop it. They might set up a few stings and try, but it will be similar to file sharing music. So many people use it that for every one person they arrest another one million folks will have downloaded music.

Just search for Bit Coin, Silk Road and Tor and you will figure the rest out.

The other black market occupations I discussed are wonderful ways to stay off the books. One thing to remember is if you're washing dogs for a living and then there are no more dogs to be washed, you're more likely to be eating dog food than raking in the dough, without a back-up plan. If you're going to be an active part of the underground economy, you probably want to have more than one source of income.

Chapter 6:

Final Thoughts

Use some common sense in your transition to an Agorist lifestyle. If you're reading this, you're probably starting to get a little bit excited about launching yourself beyond the reach of the state, and I really have to encourage you to keep both feet on the ground! Don't quit your job yet! I know the reason you're interested in starting a black market business is that you can't stand your boss, you've had enough, etc., but you can't just stop working without completely destroying your life. You have to ease into this. It doesn't mean you can't make this transition or that you can't sometimes do it quickly. You may be able to. I've seen it happen.

I have a buddy who makes baklava out of his house, and when he started to devote real time to it, within a few months he'd already paid off his credit cards, and if he keeps at it, he'll probably make at least enough to live comfortably, if not exceed his previous "regular" income. He has one of the greatest quotes of all time: "It's sad, and speaks to today's society, that cooking and selling baklava out of your house is now considered activism." It really puts things in perspective, when in this country you can't even cook and sell food out of your house without it being an act of civil disobedience.

In the end, my friend is a great example for anyone wanting to start a black market business: he did something. And you can too. Just keep your normal job, and start a side job on the weekends. Go to the flea markets, start a dog washing business, cut hair, anything to find a need and fill it. Keep building this second, side job, and begin thinking about what your tipping point should be. Have a threshold at which point you can say,

"Ok, I'm making this much money, I can now give up my regular job." And then, again, transition into it.

Make sure, as well, that you keep cash close to you and on hand, so that no-one can raid a bank account, coerce you into paying fines, sue you, or glance at your books and know you've got money. It's extremely difficult to collect money from people that don't have money in bank accounts. How do I know this? I used to be a landlord with some rental properties and I had people dead-to-rights who had come in, trashed the place, racked up thousands of dollars in owed rent and damages. I sued them, had a judgment against them, but was unable to collect that money. You simply can't collect money from a dead-beat if they don't have money on the books. Unlike my irresponsible deadbeat tenants, you can use this information consciously and to your advantage.

We live in a messed up society. You and your actions can be declared illegal just because you have the guts to stand up for what's right and dare to make a living without a politician's or bureaucrat's blessing. It's precisely because our society is so messed up that I don't have any qualms teaching you how to beat their system. Go ahead and let them try to find you. Good luck collecting any money! If you minimize risk with the methods I've suggested, you should be able to shelter yourself from the iron fist of government. Even if you own your house (which might typically be imperiled and threatened as an asset, were the government to catch on to your black market business), there are ways of moving such assets out of being held in your own name. And if your business isn't held in your name, that's even safer, as I explained before. Even if they put liens on your home, you can refuse to sell your home to satisfy the liens. If you intend to spend the rest of your life in that house, don't worry about it. It's just fines and money. If you don't buy into the fear, there's really not much they can do. To review, it's always safer not to own anything on paper.

Lastly, a good way to protect your privacy is to use one of the many electronic resources available today. You can go buy a cell phone at a store and never have to show an ID. It does not take long to find a no contract company and use that.

Just start something and get your feet wet. The only way to begin a black market business is to get off your butt and try it. After you shut this book, you should be sitting with a list you've made as you went along, saying, "This is what I do well," or "I have no skills, but I like some of these ideas, maybe I'll pick one like buying and selling from Craigslist to eBay," or "...maybe I'll learn how to buy wholesale and sell at the flea market."

Use these ideas to your advantage. And remember to connect with other agorists operating their own businesses. Other black market businesses will promote yours and help you, if you do the same for them. You have to help your friends survive. Be honest. Show people you care about them. That's the way you build a business.

My customers buy from me, even though they could buy somewhere else and at a lower price, because I care about them. I love my customers. I take care of them. They're my friends. They know that I'm trying to do this for reasons that are bigger than I am. It's about liberty. It's not just me making a buck. These are the types of activists that you want to be friends with. And you can find them pretty easily, especially online. You can find me at http://LupoLit.com . Please help me out and share this book, it is only a 99 cent eBook. That is a steal for this life changing information.

So, get out there and do it! Start a whole new life for yourself. Within a short time, hopefully you'll be well on your way to a life outside the system where you can be proud of what you are and what you do. As always, good hunting!

~ Tarrin P. Lupo

Some of the Resources Mentioned

LCL Report – http://youtube.com/lclreport

eBay

Skype

PayPal

Bitcoin

ClickBank.com

SiteBuildIt.com

Facebook

MySpace

MeetUp

Craigslist

SmashWords

CreateSpace

Amazon

Flea markets

Immigrant communities

Classifieds